GETTING STARTED

Gardening is a fun activity you can do all-year round. Perhaps you'd like to grow beautiful flowers, or some tasty fruit and vegetables. There are so many amazing plants to choose from!

This book is full of projects for every budding gardener. It will guide you through what you need to get started, along with ten fun gardening projects you can do at home.

Remember, you don't need a garden to get into gardening. All you need is a bit of indoor space, such as a warm, sunny window-sill.

Many plants grow best from seeds, which you can buy at a garden centre or a market. But we've included some seedless activities too, along with top tips and techniques to make sure that your plants flourish.

It's time to get into gardening!

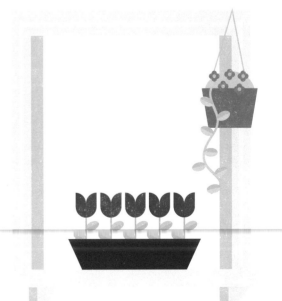

SEEDS AND SEEDLINGS

Plants produce seeds that grow into new plants. Each plant produces its own kind of seed. They come in all shapes and sizes!

Keep the soil moist to the touch throughout your plant's life, but not dripping or soaking. If you add too much water, make sure it can drain away.

Seeds need four things to grow into plants:

- Warmth
- Light
- Something to grow in
- Water

Warmth and light are easy. A sunny indoor window-sill is perfect!

Most young plants grow best in a type of soil mix called potting compost. You can buy this at your local garden centre or DIY shop.

get into

GARDENING

growing projects for window-sill and garden!

judith heneghan

WAYLAND

CONTENTS

HOW SEEDS GROW

STEP 1
Water helps the hard, outer shell of the seed to soften. Warmth tells the seed that it is time to germinate and grow.

STEP 2
Soon, a tiny root appears. The root grows down and holds the new plant steady in the soil. It also takes in water and nutrients from the soil.

STEP 3
Next, a shoot appears. The shoot grows up towards the light. Now, the seed has become a seedling.

STEP 4
As the seedling grows, it sends out green leaves.

STEP 5
When the plant is fully grown, it produces a flower.

STEP 6
This flower produces new seeds, which disperse when the flower wilts.

WHAT YOU NEED

Gardening equipment doesn't have to be fancy. You probably have some of these items at home already!

Stakes and ties for supporting tall plants

Labels made from strips of plastic yoghurt pot or wooden lollipop sticks

Potting compost

Foil trays, saucers or some folded newspaper to place under containers

Water from a jug or small watering can

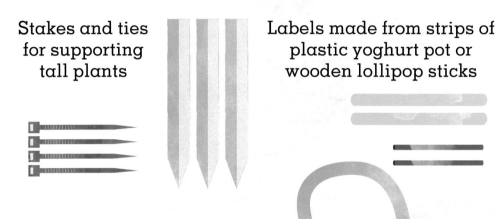

Containers with small holes in the bottom

Garden rake, for raking garden soil and getting rid of lumps.

Trowels and forks are useful for working with soil.

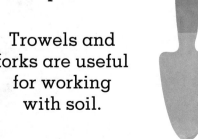

MAKING HOLES

If you are gardening indoors or on a patio, your soil will need a container. This should have a few small holes in the bottom so that extra water can drain away.

A plastic yoghurt pot can be used again and again. Wash it first, then make 2–3 small holes in the bottom.

Cardboard egg boxes make perfect pots for young seedlings. Push a toothpick through the base to make some holes.

Always ask an adult to make holes in plastic containers for you – they can use screwdrivers or skewers.

Try cutting the bottom off a clear plastic soda bottle or milk carton. Don't forget to make some holes!

Don't forget: if you're using a holey container, you'll need a saucer or tray to put it on.

You can decorate the container with paints or felt tips. Or, try placing it inside your favourite mug or bowl.

BRIGHT NASTURTIUMS

Nasturtiums are cheerful, easy-to-grow plants with interesting leaves and orange or red flowers. They look great in a pot on a window-sill, or in a container outside.

STEP 1

Fill your pot with compost until it is three-quarters full. Moisten with water all the way through.

STEP 2

Poke your finger into the soil, up to your second finger joint, to make a narrow hole. Drop a single seed into the hole and lightly cover with soil.

STEP 3

Place the pot on a saucer and put it in a warm, sunny place, such as a window-sill. Keep the compost moist to the touch, but not dripping wet.

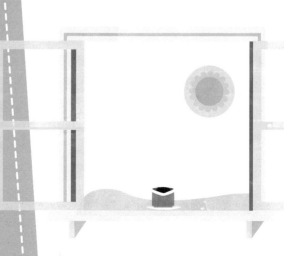

YOU WILL NEED

Packet of nasturtium seeds

Watering can

Trowel

Saucer

Yoghurt-sized pot with drainage holes

Potting compost

STEP 4

After 10–14 days, a seedling should appear. Turn the pot each day so that each side has equal amounts of sunshine.

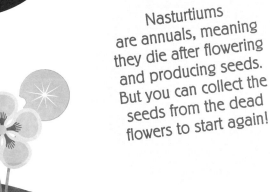

Nasturtiums are annuals, meaning they die after flowering and producing seeds. But you can collect the seeds from the dead flowers to start again!

STEP 6

When each flower dies, remove it by pinching the top of its stem. This helps new flowers appear.

STEP 5

As the plant grows, let its leaves tumble down the sides of the pot. After about eight weeks, the first flowers should appear.

PRETTY PANSIES

Pansy seeds are also easy to grow from seed. They come in all kinds of colours!

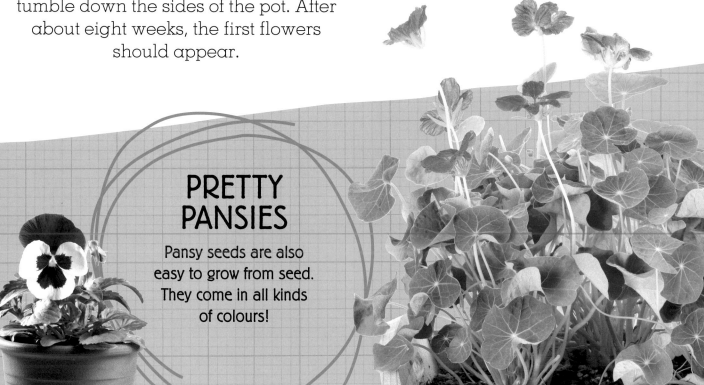

SIMPLE SALAD

A box of freshly grown salad is a tasty treat! The best time to plant the seeds is in the spring or early autumn.

YOU WILL NEED

Packet of mixed green salad seeds

Scissors   Trowel

Watering can

Tray to sit the container on

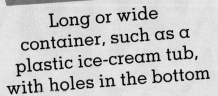

Long or wide container, such as a plastic ice-cream tub, with holes in the bottom

Potting compost

STEP 1

Almost fill your container with potting compost and sprinkle it thoroughly with water until the compost is moist all the way through. Sprinkle the seeds evenly across the surface. Cover with a thin layer of compost.

STEP 2

Place the container on a bright window-sill, but avoid strong heat. Keep the compost moist!

STEP 3

When the seedlings are about 3 cm high, thin them out so they are about 10 cm apart.

If your seedlings grow very close together, they soon become overcrowded. Removing the smaller seedlings will help. This is called 'thinning out'.

STEP 5

Snip off and eat the outside leaves of each plant. Their smaller, inner leaves will continue to grow!

STEP 4

The salad leaves are ready to eat when they are about 10 cm high. This takes around six weeks.

ROCKET POWER

Try growing some rocket leaves to add to your salad. Rocket has a peppery flavour that's delicious mixed with other leaves!

TASTY HERBS

Herbs grow well in medium-sized pots and look great on a sunny window-sill. They smell good and taste delicious! Best of all, you can grow them throughout the year.

STEP 1

Fill each pot almost to the top with some compost, then water them carefully.

STEP 2

Sprinkle a few seeds of your first chosen herb on top of one pot and add a label with the herb's name. Cover your seeds lightly with a thin layer of compost, then repeat for the other pots.

YOU WILL NEED

Herb seeds, such as basil, chives and mint

Watering can

Saucer or tray

Trowel

Potting compost

Medium-sized containers, such as round ice-cream tubs or clay pots, with holes

Labels

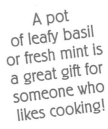

A pot of leafy basil or fresh mint is a great gift for someone who likes cooking!

STEP 3

Put your pots on a warm, sunny window-sill. Keep the compost moist but not soggy.

STEP 4

After 4–6 weeks, you should have enough leaves to pinch off a handful. The herbs will keep growing if some leaves remain on the plant.

STEP 5

Try basil on pasta, chives with baby potatoes, and chopped mint in a fruit salad. Yum!

CURLY CORIANDER

There are lots of herbs to try. Coriander is easy to grow and just as delicious!

MINI-SPIDERS

Spider plants are easy to grow indoors. You don't have to grow one from seed; all you need is an adult spider plant that has sprouted a mini-spider! A mini-spider is called a spiderette.

STEP 1

Choose a spiderette growing from an adult spider plant. Using the scissors, snip it off at the bottom of the long shoot.

YOU WILL NEED

Adult spider plant that has sprouted spiderettes

Trowel   Scissors

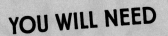

Potting compost

Saucer

Small glass jar

Watering can

Medium-sized pot with holes in the bottom

STEP 2

Place the spiderette in a jar of water. The jar should be full enough that the spiderette's leaves rest on the jar's rim. Place the jar on a bright window-sill. Change the water every couple of days.

You can grow dozens of new spider plants from one parent plant. Give some to your friends!

STEP 3

After two weeks, when the roots have grown to about 7–8 cm long, prepare a container by filling it two-thirds full with moist compost.

STEP 4

Remove the spiderette from the water and place it in the container. Add some more compost around the base of the plant.

STEP 5

Keep the compost moist, and make sure the plant stays out of intense sunlight. Now you have a new spider plant to care for!

GORGEOUS GERANIUMS

Grow a baby geranium, too! Cut off a stubby stem from an adult geranium and plant it in a pot of moist compost. After four weeks, it should grow new roots.

SUPER STRAWBERRIES
TRANSPLANTING

Strawberry plants develop fruit when insects spread pollen from one flower to another. So, your plants need to move outside; a sunny patio or balcony is perfect. Strawberry plants also grow well in hanging baskets that are sheltered from the wind.

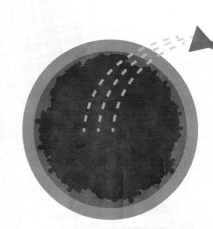

STEP 1
Fill your pot with compost, then water it thoroughly.

STEP 2
Push your forefinger into the compost to make a narrow hole. Do this 5–6 times, with each hole spaced about 8 cm apart.

YOU WILL NEED

50-cm wide, 15-cm deep container, with holes

Trowel

Potting compost

Egg box full of strawberry seedlings

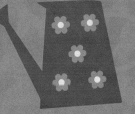

Watering can

STEP 3
Hold the stem of a seedling between your thumb and forefinger and pull, gently, until the roots are free of the compost.

STEP 4
Lower the roots into a hole in the large container, then pat compost around it. Repeat until you have transplanted 5–6 seedlings.

STEP 5
While it's still chilly, only put the container outside on sunny days; remember to bring it in at night! When there is no more chance of frost, you can leave the plants out permanently. In a few weeks, your strawberries will be ready to eat!

The seedlings you've grown in egg boxes will need to adjust to the outdoor temperature. This is called 'hardening off'.

SMALL AND SWEET
Try growing alpine strawberries for smaller, more dainty fruit with a deliciously sweet taste!

GLORIOUS SUNFLOWERS

Why not take the sunflower challenge with your friends? See who can grow the tallest sunflower!

Sunflowers are the giants of the garden – some varieties grow to 3 m tall! You can plant the seeds indoors but, sooner or later, they'll have to go outside.

YOU WILL NEED

Large yoghurt pots with holes

Garden stakes at least 1.5 m tall

Sunflower seeds

Watering can

Trowel

Ties

Potting compost

STEP 1

In March, fill a yoghurt pot with mo[i] compost, then make a shallow hol[e] in the centre. Place one sunflower seed inside. Repeat for further seed[s] giving each one its own pot.

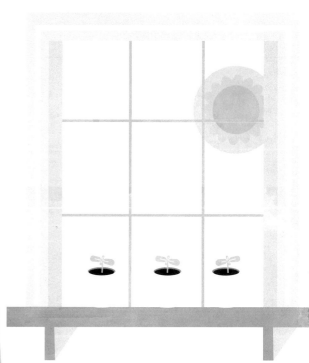

STEP 2

Place the pots on a sunny window-sill. After three weeks, seedlings should appear.

STEP 3

Harden off the seedlings gradually. Remember, that means putting the pots outside on nice sunny days and bringing them inside at night. When all danger of frost has passed, use a trowel to dig holes at least 60 cm apart in some soil outside, beside a sunny, sheltered fence or wall.

STEP 4

Using the same method as on pages 22–23, transplant each young sunflower into a separate hole. Cover the roots with plenty of soil.

STEP 5

When the plants reach 50 cm tall, push a stake into the soil, 6–7 cm away from each stem. Then tie a stake to each stem to stop it falling over. Huge yellow flowers will bloom in late summer.

EASY PEASY

If you like tall outdoor plants, try growing sweet peas! Plant the seeds indoors, harden them off, transplant them into the garden and support them with stakes in the same way. Sweet peas are not edible, despite their name.

CRUNCHY CARROTS

Carrots are easy to grow outdoors. You can sow the seeds straight into the ground in April. Then dig up your crop of tasty carrots in July and August!

STEP 1

Dig up any weeds. Then, rake your patch of garden soil until you have a flat, even area with no big stones or lumps. If the soil is dry, water it.

STEP 2

Using your trowel, make a 1-cm groove in the soil in a straight line.

STEP 3

Carrot seeds are tiny! Using your thumb and forefinger, sow them evenly along the groove.

YOU WILL NEED

Watering can

Rake

Trowel

Labels

Patch of garden soil

Carrot seeds

carrots

Young carrots may be damaged by attacks from an insect called carrot fly. You can protect your carrots by covering them with some insect-proof netting, available in most garden centres.

STEP 4

Cover the seeds lightly with moist soil. Label the row, so you will remember what you've planted and where.

STEP 5

When a few leaves start to show, thin out the seedlings using the method on pages 10–11. The seedlings should be 5 cm apart.

STEP 6

Your carrots will be ready to dig up and eat when you can see their orange tops poking above the soil.

GO POTTY

You can also grow carrots in containers. Choose a short-rooted variety, and make sure your container is deep enough for the roots to develop.

INDEX

First published in Great Britain in 2016 by Wayland

Copyright © Wayland, 2016

All rights reserved.

Author: Judith Heneghan
Editor: Liza Miller
Illustration: Ana Djordjevic
Designer: Simon Daley

ISBN: 978 0 7502 9846 9

10 9 8 7 6 5 4 3 2 1

Wayland
An imprint of
Hachette Children's Group
Part of Hodder & Stoughton
Carmelite House
50 Victoria Embankment
London EC4Y 0DZ

An Hachette UK Company
www.hachette.co.uk
www.hachettechildrens.co.uk

Printed in China

The website addresses (URLs) included in this book were valid at the time of going to press. However, it is possible that contents or addresses may have changed since the publication of this book. No responsibility for any such changes can be accepted by either the author or the Publisher.

Picture acknowledgements: The Publisher would like to thank the following for permission to reproduce their pictures. Via Dreamstime: p 11 bl Marilyn Barbone. Via Shutterstock: p 4 Madlen; p 9 br TAGSTOCK1; p 9 bl giulianax; p 11 br Doglikehorse p 13 br Eskymaks; p 13 bl marilyn barbone; p 15 br fotoknips; p 15 bl Neirfy; p 17 br Moving Moment; p 17 bl Peter Zijlstra; p 19 br TCGraphicDesign; p 19 bl Marina Lohrbach; p 23 br Wolna; p 23 bl Potapov Alexander; p 25 br Melinda Fawver; p 25 bl Tatiana Volgutova; p 27 br Diana Taliun; p 27 bl DenisNata; p 29 br Anna Morgan; p 29 bl Neirfy.